PHILIPPIANS

Choosing Joy

LOVEGODGREATLY.COM

A Word to Parents

This book grew out of a desire to provide a companion study journal for children for use alongside the *Philippians - Choosing Joy* adult study journal and book.

Love God Greatly is dedicated to making God's Word available to our beautiful community of women... and now, women have the opportunity to share God's Word with children through this study uniquely crafted for young hearts.

CONTENTS

INTRODUCTION

PHILIPPIANS

Hey everyone... welcome to our study of the book of Philippians! In case you didn't know, Philippians is actually a letter written to the Christians in Philippi, a place that Paul visited on his second missionary journey. Here's an interesting fact: Philippi was named after Philip of Macedonia, the father of Alexander the Great!

This letter has a very relaxed tone, giving us the picture that Paul was close to the people there. It is clear these believers have a special place in his heart.

Philippians is a favorite book for many because of its emphasis on joy, mixed with an uplifting and encouraging tone. This is pretty amazing considering it was written by Paul while he was in prison. These four chapters show us that the power of the Lord has the ability to make us rise above our circumstances and experience joy, contentment, and love for others. Speaking of joy, have you ever sung the song, "I've got the joy, joy, joy, joy down in my heart..."? It's a children's Sunday school song, and whenever I read Philippians this song pops into my head! Go ahead and sing it now if you'd like!

Joy is a main theme in this letter. Since Paul mentions it about 17 times, it is something that deserves our great attention. But how is it possible to have deep joy in the midst of overwhelming sorrow and suffering? Paul is not only a great example to us, but he also points us to the answer. Philippians has 104 verses and Jesus is mentioned directly or indirectly 51 times. That says a lot about what the ultimate theme of this book is. In the end Paul will teach us that greater than joy is Jesus: the Author of our joy.

Without Jesus there is no salvation, and therefore no lasting joy. Without Jesus there is no way to overcome our circumstances, to love people who are hard to love, to make peace, to forgive, and to live godly lives.

Augustine said, "Where your pleasure is, there is your treasure; Where your treasure is, there is your heart; Where your heart is, there is your happiness."

Let's open our Bibles and seek to better know our Savior and the joy he offers to those who follow him.

"THESE THINGS I HAVE SPOKEN TO YOU, THAT MY JOY MAY BE IN YOU, AND THAT YOUR JOY MAY BE FULL."

JOHN 15:11

READING PLAN

WEEK 1

Joy in suffering

Monday
READ: Philippians 1:1-6 • SOAP: 1:6

Tuesday
READ: Philippians 1:7-11 • SOAP: 1:9-11

Wednesday
READ: Philippians 1:12-14 • SOAP: 1:14

Thursday
READ: Philippians 1:15-18 • SOAP: 1:18

Friday
READ: Philippians 1:19-30 • SOAP: 1:21, 27

WEEK 2

Joy in serving

Monday
READ: Philippians 2:1-4 • SOAP: 2:3-4

Tuesday
READ: Philippians 2:5-11 • SOAP: 2:9-11

Wednesday
READ: Philippians 2:12-13 • SOAP: 2:13

Thursday
READ: Philippians 2:14-18 • SOAP: 2:14-16

Friday
READ: Philippians 2:19-30 • SOAP: 2:20-21

WEEK 3

Joy in believing

Monday
READ: Philippians 3:1-4 • SOAP: 3:3

Tuesday
READ: Philippians 3:5-11 • SOAP: 3:8-9

Wednesday
READ: Philippians 3:12-14 • SOAP: 3:12-14

Thursday
READ: Philippians 3:15-19 • SOAP: 3:16

Friday
READ: Philippians 3:20-21 • SOAP: 3:20

WEEK 4

Joy in giving

Monday
READ: Philippians 4:1-5 • SOAP: 4:4-5

Tuesday
READ: Philippians 4:6-7 • SOAP: 4:6-7

Wednesday
READ: Philippians 4:8-9 • SOAP: 4:8

Thursday
READ: Philippians 4:10-13 • SOAP: 4:12-13

Friday
READ: Philippians 4:14-23 • SOAP: 4:19

YOUR GOALS

We believe it's important to write out goals for this study. Take some time now and write three goals you would like to focus on as you begin to rise each day and dig into God's Word. Make sure and refer back to these goals throughout the next four weeks to help you stay focused. You can do it!

1.

2.

3.

Signature:

Date:

PRAYER

WRITE DOWN YOUR PRAYER REQUESTS AND PRAISES FOR EACH DAY.

Prayer focus for this week:
Spend time praying for your family members.

MONDAY

TUESDAY

WEDNESDAY

THURSDAY

FRIDAY

WEEK 1
Joy in suffering

And it is my prayer that your love may

abound more and more, with knowledge

and all discernment, so that you may

approve what is excellent,

and so be pure and blameless

for the day of Christ,

Philippians 1:9-10

SCRIPTURE FOR WEEK 1

MONDAY

Philippians 1:1-6

1 Paul and Timothy, servants of Christ Jesus,

To all the saints in Christ Jesus who are at Philippi, with the overseers and deacons:

2 Grace to you and peace from God our Father and the Lord Jesus Christ.

3 I thank my God in all my remembrance of you, 4 always in every prayer of mine for you all making my prayer with joy, 5 because of your partnership in the gospel from the first day until now. 6 And I am sure of this, that he who began a good work in you will bring it to completion at the day of Jesus Christ.

TUESDAY

Philippians 1:7-11

7 It is right for me to feel this way about you all, because I hold you in my heart, for you are all partakers with me of grace, both in my imprisonment and in the defense and confirmation of the gospel. 8 For God is my witness, how I yearn for you all with the affection of Christ Jesus. 9 And it is my prayer that your love may abound more and more, with knowledge and all discernment, 10 so that you may approve what is excellent, and so be pure and blameless for the day of Christ, 11 filled with the fruit of righteousness that comes through Jesus Christ, to the glory and praise of God.

WEDNESDAY

Philippians 1:12-14

12 I want you to know, brothers, that what has happened to me has really served to advance the gospel, 13 so that it has become known throughout the whole imperial guard and to all the rest that my imprisonment is for Christ. 14 And most of the brothers, having become confident in the Lord by my imprisonment, are much more bold to speak the word without fear.

THURSDAY

Philippians 1:15-18

15 Some indeed preach Christ from envy and rivalry, but others from good will.16 The latter do it out of love, knowing that I am put here for the defense of the gospel. 17 The former proclaim Christ out of selfish ambition, not sincerely but thinking to afflict me in my imprisonment. 18 What then? Only that in every way, whether in pretense or in truth, Christ is proclaimed, and in that I rejoice. Yes, and I will rejoice,

FRIDAY

Philippians 1:19-30

19 for I know that through your prayers and the help of the Spirit of Jesus Christ this will turn out for my deliverance, 20 as it is my eager expectation and hope that I will not be at all ashamed, but that with full courage now as always Christ will be honored in my body, whether by life or by death.21 For to me to live is Christ, and to die is gain. 22 If I am to live in the flesh, that means fruitful labor for me. Yet which I shall choose I cannot tell. 23 I am hard pressed between the two. My desire is to depart and be with Christ, for that is far better. 24 But to remain in the flesh is more necessary on your account.25 Convinced of this, I know that I will remain and continue with you all, for your progress and joy in the faith, 26 so that in me you may have ample cause to glory in Christ Jesus, because of my coming to you again.

27 Only let your manner of life be worthy of the gospel of Christ, so that whether I come and see you or am absent, I may hear of you that you are standing firm in one spirit, with one mind striving side by side for the faith of the gospel, 28 and not frightened in anything by your opponents. This is a clear sign to them of their destruction, but of your salvation, and that from God. 29 For it has been granted to you that for the sake of Christ you should not only believe in him but also suffer for his sake, 30 engaged in the same conflict that you saw I had and now hear that I still have.

MONDAY

READ:
Philippians 1:1-6
SOAP:
Philippians 1:6

1. Write out today's **SCRIPTURE** passage.

_____

_____

_____

_____

_____

_____

_____

_____

_____

_____

2. On the blank page to the right, **DRAW** or **WRITE** what this passage means to you.

3. My **PRAYER** for today:

_____

_____

_____

_____

_____

TUESDAY

READ:
Philippians 1:7-11
SOAP:
Philippians 1:9-11

1. Write out today's **SCRIPTURE** passage.

_____

_____

_____

_____

_____

_____

_____

_____

_____

_____

2. On the blank page to the right, **DRAW** or **WRITE** what this passage means to you.

3. My **PRAYER** for today:

_____

_____

_____

_____

_____

WEDNESDAY

READ:
Philippians 1:12-14
SOAP:
Philippians 1:14

1. Write out today's **SCRIPTURE** passage.

_____

_____

_____

_____

_____

_____

_____

_____

_____

_____

2. On the blank page to the right, **DRAW** or **WRITE** what this passage means to you.

3. My **PRAYER** for today:

_____

_____

_____

_____

_____

THURSDAY

READ:
Philippians 1:15-18
SOAP:
Philippians 1:18

1. Write out today's **SCRIPTURE** passage.

_____

_____

_____

_____

_____

_____

_____

_____

_____

_____

2. On the blank page to the right, **DRAW** or **WRITE** what this passage means to you.

3. My **PRAYER** for today:

_____

_____

_____

_____

_____

FRIDAY

READ:
Philippians 1:19-30
SOAP:
Philippians 1:21, 27

1. Write out today's **SCRIPTURE** passage.

_____

_____

_____

_____

_____

_____

_____

_____

_____

_____

2. On the blank page to the right, **DRAW** or **WRITE** what this passage means to you.

3. My **PRAYER** for today:

_____

_____

_____

_____

_____

THIS WEEK I LEARNED...

USE THE SPACE BELOW TO DRAW A PICTURE OR WRITE
ABOUT WHAT YOU LEARNED THIS WEEK FROM YOUR
TIME IN GOD'S WORD.

PRAYER

WRITE DOWN YOUR PRAYER REQUESTS AND PRAISES FOR EACH DAY.

Prayer focus for this week:
Spend time praying for your country.

MONDAY

TUESDAY

WEDNESDAY

THURSDAY

FRIDAY

WEEK 2
Joy in serving

Do nothing from
selfish ambition or conceit,
but in humility count others
more significant than yourselves.

Philippians 2:3

SCRIPTURE FOR WEEK 2

MONDAY

Philippians 2:1-4

1 So if there is any encouragement in Christ, any comfort from love, any participation in the Spirit, any affection and sympathy, 2 complete my joy by being of the same mind, having the same love, being in full accord and of one mind. 3 Do nothing from selfish ambition or conceit, but in humility count others more significant than yourselves. 4 Let each of you look not only to his own interests, but also to the interests of others.

TUESDAY

Philippians 2:5-11

5 Have this mind among yourselves, which is yours in Christ Jesus, 6 who, though he was in the form of God, did not count equality with God a thing to be grasped, 7 but emptied himself, by taking the form of a servant, being born in the likeness of men. 8 And being found in human form, he humbled himself by becoming obedient to the point of death, even death on a cross. 9 Therefore God has highly exalted him and bestowed on him the name that is above every name, 10 so that at the name of Jesus every knee should bow, in heaven and on earth and under the earth, 11 and every tongue confess that Jesus Christ is Lord, to the glory of God the Father.

WEDNESDAY

Philippians 2:12-13

12 Therefore, my beloved, as you have always obeyed, so now, not only as in my presence but much more in my absence, work out your own salvation with fear and trembling, 13 for it is God who works in you, both to will and to work for his good pleasure.

THURSDAY

Philippians 2:14-18

14 Do all things without grumbling or disputing, 15 that you may be blameless and innocent, children of God without blemish in the midst of a crooked and twisted generation, among whom you shine as lights in the world, 16 holding fast to the word of life, so that in the day of Christ I may be proud that I did not run in vain or labor in vain. 17 Even if I am to be poured out as a drink offering upon the sacrificial offering of your faith, I am glad and rejoice with you all. 18 Likewise you also should be glad and rejoice with me.

FRIDAY

Philippians 2:19-30

19 I hope in the Lord Jesus to send Timothy to you soon, so that I too may be cheered by news of you. 20 For I have no one like him, who will be genuinely concerned for your welfare. 21 For they all seek their own interests, not those of Jesus Christ. 22 But you know Timothy's proven worth, how as a son with a father he has served with me in the gospel. 23 I hope therefore to send him just as soon as I see how it will go with me, 24 and I trust in the Lord that shortly I myself will come also.

25 I have thought it necessary to send to you Epaphroditus my brother and fellow worker and fellow soldier, and your messenger and minister to my need, 26 for he has been longing for you all and has been distressed because you heard that he was ill. 27 Indeed he was ill, near to death. But God had mercy on him, and not only on him but on me also, lest I should have sorrow upon sorrow. 28 I am the more eager to send him, therefore, that you may rejoice at seeing him again, and that I may be less anxious. 29 So receive him in the Lord with all joy, and honor such men, 30 for he nearly died for the work of Christ, risking his life to complete what was lacking in your service to me.

MONDAY

READ:
Philippians 2:1-4
SOAP:
Philippians 2:3-4

1. Write out today's **SCRIPTURE** passage.

_____

_____

_____

_____

_____

_____

_____

_____

_____

_____

2. On the blank page to the right, **DRAW** or **WRITE** what this passage means to you.

3. My **PRAYER** for today:

_____

_____

_____

_____

_____

TUESDAY

READ:
Philippians 2:5-11
SOAP:
Philippians 2:9-11

1. Write out today's **SCRIPTURE** passage.

_____

_____

_____

_____

_____

_____

_____

_____

_____

_____

2. On the blank page to the right, **DRAW** or **WRITE** what this passage means to you.

3. My **PRAYER** for today:

_____

_____

_____

_____

_____

WEDNESDAY

READ:
Philippians 2:12-13
SOAP:
Philippians 2:13

1. Write out today's **SCRIPTURE** passage.

_____

_____

_____

_____

_____

_____

_____

_____

_____

_____

2. On the blank page to the right, **DRAW** or **WRITE** what this passage means to you.

3. My **PRAYER** for today:

_____

_____

_____

_____

_____

THURSDAY

READ:
Philippians 2:14-18

SOAP:
Philippians 2:14-16

1. Write out today's **SCRIPTURE** passage.

_____

_____

_____

_____

_____

_____

_____

_____

_____

2. On the blank page to the right, **DRAW** or **WRITE** what this passage means to you.

3. My **PRAYER** for today:

_____

_____

_____

_____

_____

FRIDAY

READ:
Philippians 2:19-30

SOAP:
Philippians 2:20-21

1. Write out today's **SCRIPTURE** passage.

_____

_____

_____

_____

_____

_____

_____

_____

_____

_____

2. On the blank page to the right, **DRAW** or **WRITE** what this passage means to you.

3. My **PRAYER** for today:

_____

_____

_____

_____

_____

THIS WEEK I LEARNED...

USE THE SPACE BELOW TO DRAW A PICTURE OR WRITE ABOUT WHAT YOU LEARNED THIS WEEK FROM YOUR TIME IN GOD'S WORD.

PRAYER

WRITE DOWN YOUR PRAYER REQUESTS AND PRAISES FOR EACH DAY.

Prayer focus for this week:
Spend time praying for your friends.

MONDAY

TUESDAY

WEDNESDAY

THURSDAY

FRIDAY

WEEK 3
Joy in believing

Indeed, I count everything as loss
because of the surpassing worth of
knowing Christ Jesus my Lord. For his
sake I have suffered the loss of all things
and count them as rubbish, in order that
I may gain Christ

Philippians 3:8

SCRIPTURE FOR WEEK 3

MONDAY

Philippians 3:1-4

1 Finally, my brothers, rejoice in the Lord. To write the same things to you is no trouble to me and is safe for you.

2 Look out for the dogs, look out for the evildoers, look out for those who mutilate the flesh. 3 For we are the circumcision, who worship by the Spirit of God and glory in Christ Jesus and put no confidence in the flesh— 4 though I myself have reason for confidence in the flesh also. If anyone else thinks he has reason for confidence in the flesh, I have more:

TUESDAY

Philippians 3:5-11

5 circumcised on the eighth day, of the people of Israel, of the tribe of Benjamin, a Hebrew of Hebrews; as to the law, a Pharisee; 6 as to zeal, a persecutor of the church; as to righteousness under the law, blameless. 7 But whatever gain I had, I counted as loss for the sake of Christ. 8 Indeed, I count everything as loss because of the surpassing worth of knowing Christ Jesus my Lord. For his sake I have suffered the loss of all things and count them as rubbish, in order that I may gain Christ 9 and be found in him, not having a righteousness of my own that comes from the law, but that which comes through faith in Christ, the righteousness from God that depends on faith— 10 that I may know him and the power of his resurrection, and may share his sufferings, becoming like him in his death, 11 that by any means possible I may attain the resurrection from the dead.

WEDNESDAY

Philippians 3:12-14

12 Not that I have already obtained this or am already perfect, but I press on to make it my own, because Christ Jesus has made me his own. 13 Brothers, I do not consider that I have made it my own. But one thing I do: forgetting what lies behind and straining forward to what lies ahead, 14 I press on toward the goal for the prize of the upward call of God in Christ Jesus.

THURSDAY

Philippians 3:15-19

15 Let those of us who are mature think this way, and if in anything you think otherwise, God will reveal that also to you. 16 Only let us hold true to what we have attained.

17 Brothers, join in imitating me, and keep your eyes on those who walk according to the example you have in us. 18 For many, of whom I have often told you and now tell you even with tears, walk as enemies of the cross of Christ. 19 Their end is destruction, their god is their belly, and they glory in their shame, with minds set on earthly things.

FRIDAY

Philippians 3:20-21

20 But our citizenship is in heaven, and from it we await a Savior, the Lord Jesus Christ, 21 who will transform our lowly body to be like his glorious body, by the power that enables him even to subject all things to himself.

MONDAY

READ:
Philippians 3:1-4
SOAP:
Philippians 3:3

1. Write out today's **SCRIPTURE** passage.

_____

_____

_____

_____

_____

_____

_____

_____

_____

_____

2. On the blank page to the right, **DRAW** or **WRITE** what this passage means to you.

3. My **PRAYER** for today:

_____

_____

_____

_____

_____

TUESDAY

READ:
Philippians 3:5-11
SOAP:
Philippians 3:8-9

1. Write out today's **SCRIPTURE** passage.

_____

_____

_____

_____

_____

_____

_____

_____

_____

_____

2. On the blank page to the right, **DRAW** or **WRITE** what this passage means to you.

3. My **PRAYER** for today:

_____

_____

_____

_____

_____

WEDNESDAY

READ:
Philippians 3:12-14
SOAP:
Philippians 3:12-14

1. Write out today's **SCRIPTURE** passage.

_____

_____

_____

_____

_____

_____

_____

_____

_____

_____

2. On the blank page to the right, **DRAW** or **WRITE** what this passage means to you.

3. My **PRAYER** for today:

_____

_____

_____

_____

_____

THURSDAY

READ:
Philippians 3:15-19
SOAP:
Philippians 3:16

1. Write out today's **SCRIPTURE** passage.

_____

_____

_____

_____

_____

_____

_____

_____

_____

_____

2. On the blank page to the right, **DRAW** or **WRITE** what this passage means to you.

3. My **PRAYER** for today:

_____

_____

_____

_____

_____

_____

FRIDAY

READ:
Philippians 3:20-21
SOAP:
Philippians 3:20

1. Write out today's **SCRIPTURE** passage.

_____

_____

_____

_____

_____

_____

_____

_____

_____

_____

2. On the blank page to the right, **DRAW** or **WRITE** what this passage means to you.

3. My **PRAYER** for today:

_____

_____

_____

_____

_____

_____

THIS WEEK I LEARNED...

USE THE SPACE BELOW TO DRAW A PICTURE OR WRITE
ABOUT WHAT YOU LEARNED THIS WEEK FROM YOUR
TIME IN GOD'S WORD.

PRAYER

WRITE DOWN YOUR PRAYER REQUESTS AND PRAISES FOR EACH DAY.

Prayer focus for this week:
Spend time praying for your church.

MONDAY

TUESDAY

WEDNESDAY

THURSDAY

FRIDAY

WEEK 4

Joy in giving

Finally, brothers, whatever is true, whatever is honorable, whatever is just, whatever is pure, whatever is lovely, whatever is commendable, if there is any excellence, if there is anything worthy of praise, think about these things.

Philippians 4:8

SCRIPTURE FOR WEEK 4

MONDAY

Philippians 4:1-5

1 Therefore, my brothers, whom I love and long for, my joy and crown, stand firm thus in the Lord, my beloved.

2 I entreat Euodia and I entreat Syntyche to agree in the Lord. 3 Yes, I ask you also, true companion, help these women, who have labored side by side with me in the gospel together with Clement and the rest of my fellow workers, whose names are in the book of life.

4 Rejoice in the Lord always; again I will say, rejoice. 5 Let your reasonableness be known to everyone. The Lord is at hand;

TUESDAY

Philippians 4:6-7

6 do not be anxious about anything, but in everything by prayer and supplication with thanksgiving let your requests be made known to God. 7 And the peace of God, which surpasses all understanding, will guard your hearts and your minds in Christ Jesus.

WEDNESDAY

Philippians 4:8-9

8 Finally, brothers, whatever is true, whatever is honorable, whatever is just, whatever is pure, whatever is lovely, whatever is commendable, if there is any excellence, if there is anything worthy of praise, think about these things. 9 What you have learned and received and heard and seen in me—practice these things, and the God of peace will be with you.

THURSDAY

Philippians 4:10-13

10 I rejoiced in the Lord greatly that now at length you have revived your concern for me. You were indeed concerned for me, but you had no opportunity. 11 Not that I am speaking of being in need, for I have learned in whatever situation I am to be content. 12 I know how to be brought low, and I know how to abound. In any and every circumstance, I have learned the secret of facing plenty and hunger, abundance and need. 13 I can do all things through him who strengthens me.

FRIDAY

Philippians 4:14-23

14 Yet it was kind of you to share my trouble. 15 And you Philippians yourselves know that in the beginning of the gospel, when I left Macedonia, no church entered into partnership with me in giving and receiving, except you only. 16 Even in Thessalonica you sent me help for my needs once and again. 17 Not that I seek the gift, but I seek the fruit that increases to your credit. 18 I have received full payment, and more. I am well supplied, having received from Epaphroditus the gifts you sent, a fragrant offering, a sacrifice acceptable and pleasing to God.19 And my God will supply every need of yours according to his riches in glory in Christ Jesus. 20 To our God and Father be glory forever and ever. Amen.

21 Greet every saint in Christ Jesus. The brothers who are with me greet you. 22 All the saints greet you, especially those of Caesar's household.

23 The grace of the Lord Jesus Christ be with your spirit.

MONDAY

READ:
Philippians 4:1-5
SOAP:
Philippians 4:4-5

1. Write out today's **SCRIPTURE** passage.

_____

_____

_____

_____

_____

_____

_____

_____

_____

_____

2. On the blank page to the right, **DRAW** or **WRITE** what this passage means to you.

3. My **PRAYER** for today:

_____

_____

_____

_____

_____

TUESDAY

READ:
Philippians 4:6-7

SOAP:
Philippians 4:6-7

1. Write out today's **SCRIPTURE** passage.

_____

_____

_____

_____

_____

_____

_____

_____

_____

_____

2. On the blank page to the right, **DRAW** or **WRITE** what this passage means to you.

3. My **PRAYER** for today:

_____

_____

_____

_____

_____

WEDNESDAY

READ:
Philippians 4:8-9
SOAP:
Philippians 4:8

1. Write out today's **SCRIPTURE** passage.

_____

_____

_____

_____

_____

_____

_____

_____

_____

2. On the blank page to the right, **DRAW** or **WRITE** what this passage means to you.

3. My **PRAYER** for today:

_____

_____

_____

_____

_____

THURSDAY

READ:
Philippians 4:10-13
SOAP:
Philippians 4:12-13

1. Write out today's **SCRIPTURE** passage.

_____

_____

_____

_____

_____

_____

_____

_____

_____

_____

2. On the blank page to the right, **DRAW** or **WRITE** what this passage means to you.

3. My **PRAYER** for today:

_____

_____

_____

_____

_____

FRIDAY

READ:
Philippians 4:14-23

SOAP:
Philippians 4:19

1. Write out today's **SCRIPTURE** passage.

_____

_____

_____

_____

_____

_____

_____

_____

_____

_____

2. On the blank page to the right, **DRAW** or **WRITE** what this passage means to you.

3. My **PRAYER** for today:

_____

_____

_____

_____

_____

THIS WEEK I LEARNED...

USE THE SPACE BELOW TO DRAW A PICTURE OR WRITE ABOUT WHAT YOU LEARNED THIS WEEK FROM YOUR TIME IN GOD'S WORD.